It's Not Over Yet
I'M STILL ALIVE

It's Not Over Yet
I'M STILL ALIVE

DEDICATED TO ALL THOSE WHO WERE ALMOST FINISHED ONCE

"Ye Waqt Gujar Jayega"

Authored by
RAJESH P NAIR

Penman Books

Office No. 303, Kumar House Building,
D Block, Central Market, Opp PVR Cinema,
Prashant Vihar, Delhi 110085, India
Website: www.penmanbooks.com
Email: publish@penmanbooks.com

First Published by Penman Books 2019
Copyright © Rajesh P Nair 2019
All Rights Reserved.

Title: It's Not Over Yet, I'm Still Alive
Price: ₹699 | $ 10
ISBN: 978-93-89024-40-1

Om Hari Shree Ganapathaye Namaha

Om MahaSaraswati Namaha

Om Mahalaxmi Namaha

Om Narayanaya Namaha

Om Namah Shivaya

Mata, Pita, Guru, Daivam

Acknowledgements

I wanted to write my first book for a long time. I had various subjects in my mind. Prioritising what to write was always a confusion as I wanted to talk on many things. Once I decided on the subject, I knew that it is going to be a herculean task for me as it was my first attempt to write a book.

I take this opportunity to thank everyone who have contributed to my book directly or indirectly, as none of this would have been possible without their timely guidance, support and motivation.

At the onset, I want to thank my Mom Smt. Maniamma, Dad H/Capt. KG Purushothaman Nair and my dear Valiammachi, Smt. Omana Amma (Badi Maa) for making me capable enough to write this book. As parents they were kind enough to support me since my childhood and gave me all the love and affection in whatever I did. I want to thank my partner-in-life, Vandana (Vanita) for tolerating me over the last 20 years. My life completely changed ever since she stepped into my life. My mood swings are unbearable and she has been really kind enough. My Prince, my son, my Rishu (Rishabh), for showing me the purpose of my life. Every now and then when I look at him, I can see my reflection in everything that he does. My younger bro, Rathi (Ratheesh) for making my childhood awesome.

I would like to thank my close buddies who I go to for anything and everything in my life. Anas, Jayant and Divjot. Thank you guys for everything that you have done for me.

I would also like to thank my colleagues from the EarnWealth team for helping me complete this book on time.

Last but not the least, I would also like to thank Deepak Ji and Kailash Ji (Superfast Author) for all the learnings they passed on to me and supporting me to publish this book.

My family, my friends, and my well-wishers were always there to boost my moral, give me a push whenever I felt low, continuously behind me to make sure I stick to the decided schedule and finally help me publish it, which was the most critical step, in the whole journey.

A Big thank you to those also whose names have not been taken here. But I love you guys...

Preface

My dear friends, I would release this book on my 38th birthday, 27th Oct 2019. In the last 38 years of my living experience, I have come across many types of people. While some of them have excited me with their energy and enthusiasm, I have also seen people who never ever got excited even in good situations. While I'm a big admirer of Mahendra Singh Dhoni, the famous and most successful Indian cricket captain, for reacting seldom in both good and bad situations, I am also of the opinion that reacting to a situation and not giving-up to a situation are completely different. Some of the people who have amazed me the most are, those for whom I felt it is fully over. However, they have emerged back full-fledged and became very very successful. In your daily life you might have seen several videos on YouTube and other platforms where in the predators chase their prey and the prey escapes from the most difficult situations where you felt it's all over for them. The reason I am writing this book for you, is to share my own experiences which are real in life, happened around me where in I felt it's all over for them.

Have you ever thought, why do you give up on something that you really wanted? What forced you to quit? Why do you think it is all over? Why do you think you cannot achieve it? Why do you decide I don't want to try it again and again? Do you know that the beauty of success lies in not quitting? Why do people quit? I have seen so many people overthinking and ruining everything that they could have achieved. Personally, I have also gone through this phase during my childhood when I was a student. However, I was very lucky to have met with teachers who advised me to stop thinking and act fast.

Through this book, I want to explain you in simple words, the art of not quitting, why should you stop overthinking, how can you achieve success if you do not quit. How can you detach yourselves from addictions? How can you make your mind strong through meditation?

Happy reading, all the very best.

Contents

CHAPTER
One

Anxiety and Studies

Iwould like to dedicate this chapter to those young kids who struggle in their studies due to anxiety. This chapter is a must-read for them.

Most of us feel some anxiety from time to time, which is easily connected to situational causes. While writing this, my only Son Rishu is 10-year-old and I can easily relate to him. In this chapter, I want to explain how anxiety scrambles your brain and makes it hard to learn.

What does anxiety do to students? It causes the body to prepare itself for fight or flight.

As a parent have you ever thought why do your children get anxious? Is it too much pressure on them? Are you burning them? Is their school burning them? What is the impact of this anxiousness in their lives? Like I mentioned above, I can easily have it related with my son. He is just 10 years old. This is his age to play. He is never going to get back this period again in his life. Today if at all I miss something, I miss my childhood, I miss my school days, I miss my college days and I miss my childhood friends. I was very lucky that my parents did not put pressure on me for getting grade 1 in every exam. I was very blessed that my parents gave me a freehand to choose the time that I wanted to study. I was very blessed that I didn't had to go to early morning classes. I feel, because of all these things, I have had a good mental health during my childhood. I was never under pressure. I see so many other successful people, whom I can relate to, also have had a very cool childhood. To every student who is reading this chapter, irrespective of which class you are in, my sincere advice to you is to stop overthinking and getting anxious on your studies. If you really want to be successful, you have to enjoy the studies. I wouldn't say that, the marks that you score to get admission to the premier institutes don't impact your life. But around you, you will find a lot of successful people who are not a premier Institute pass-out. They are still doing good in their lives. So kids, if you start thinking too much about your studies, if you get anxious about your studies, if you get nervous about your studies, you are making sure that you are becoming mentally unhealthy. You are ensuring that you are getting sick. There is no need to overthink, because you overthink you cannot concentrate, you cannot enjoy the process of learning things when your brain has got the best capacity to adapt and learn things in life.

I have seen kids who got anxious about their studies, underperformed in exams, thus went into depression. You should enjoy the process of learning so that you can adapt it in your life when you grow up, so that you can pass-on whatever you have learnt to others, so that you can lead a better life. What is the use, if you learnt everything under pressure and not been able to implement it in your life because you are mentally unhealthy? I understand for me, it is very easy to say, but I have only told you things that I have adapted from my own experience. I have only told you things that I today do with my son and advise him to practice. There is no point in passing out from an IIT and IIM if you are mentally unhealthy. There is no value of that eight figure salary that you may get because you cannot enjoy your life due to the stress you are taking from your childhood.

So here comes the question of how to not overthink? What does it take to ignore overthinking and focus on things that are productive? There are different ways advised by experts. I have read many of them over the years. However, for your easy understanding, I would like to put it as seven points. I have personally advised to many students who were doing MBA and they have benefited immensely.

1. Talking to yourself in the situation of panic is one of the best ways to reduce anxiety. You must have seen this often with cricketers. All the players while batting talk to themselves to reduce their anxiety.

2. Deep breathing is another way to reduce your anxiety. I often do this. Since I practice pranayam (breathing exercise) regularly, it is the best method for me. Take a deep breath eight to ten times closing your eyes and you will find yourself relaxed.

3. Many students have told me that they get stressed after seeing huge books that they need to study to clear the exams. What I have advised them is to break coursework into small chunks. This

would require planning, but you have the option to prioritize chapters that you may like the first. However, it gives you the benefit of not leaving it all to the last minute and reduces anxiety.

4. According to the experts, procrastination is an anxious person's biggest problem. The best way to overcome this is to begin somewhere. One can easily convince himself to begin and work for just five minutes. Once you've begun you may be able to keep going. Typically, you find this helpful on items which you really don't want to do at all.

5. I must say, most of the anxious people often get hard on themselves. Here I would say, the best solution is to be kind to yourself. This doesn't mean you don't have to be disciplined. It is very easy to treat yourself bad. However, that difficult to accept that things are tough right now and think on ways how you can make things happen.

6. Many of us forget that we are not alone in this world. Everyone in this world has got some or the other problems. The only thing is that, we feel ours is the worst!!! When you talk to people, you realise that the happiest people go through the worst. This itself is a very soothing feeling. It helps you understand that your situation is not as worse as you thought.

7. One of the critical item to reduce your anxiety is to follow a healthy lifestyle. Timely eating, sleeping

and exercise can help you a lot. Just 30 minutes of simple walking a day can reduce anxiety. Indiscipline in sleeping and eating can be the worst thing that you can do to yourself.

To all the students and their overexcited parents, my sincere submission is to not overthink and spoil the mental health of your child. When I look at things as a parent, I realized that the pressure on the kids are also created by the parents. Comparing your kids with other kids in terms of talent is the biggest injustice that you can do to your children. While I understand that your intention is purely on a motivational side, you should also understand the impact it creates in the mind of your child. As a parent you play a very vital role in terms of removing this stress from your children. Bringing a grade 1 or Grade 2 or 100% marks is not an evidence that your child is going to do better in his or her life. So, it is extremely important for your children that you motivate them but not with negative comparison.

As a parent, you need to understand that your kids need some downtime in order to give their minds a much-needed rest. If you provide them quiet reflection time in the classroom, gadget-free time and some meditation periods, it can really help them overcome their anxiety. It is also important that they communicate with the same age group, make good friends and participate in games and sports. By doing all these you are helping them distract their mind from studies. It refreshes their mind and adaptability helps them to understand and learn faster.

As a Kid who is growing very fast, I want you to understand that there are many things in life which are not in your control. If you listen to motivational speakers, they would advise you that you should focus on things which are in your control. Getting anxious and taking stress on studies will only ruin things for you. While education is very important to have a successful life, you should believe in the process of learning than looking at your scores in the exam. Follow the process of learning, success would touch your feet. I advise you to see this Bollywood movie called 3 Idiots. This movie talks about the process of learning. Why you shouldn't be running behind your score cards...

Now I will tell you a real life story which happened with one of my friend's daughter. Let us name her Riya. Riya was excellent in her studies till she reached 7th standard. She always scored first grade in her class. She was also the school topper. As she entered into the high school, she started taking too much stress on her studies. Slowly, from first grade, she came down to second and then third. By the time she finished her 8th standard final exam, she was completely down. Everybody started blaming her including her parents. This poor girl had no clue on what is happening. Her parents changed her tuition teachers. By the time she finished the half term in the 9th standard, she was just an ordinary student. She went into more depression. I remember, when I spoke to her, she said that "I don't think I would pass 9th standard".

This became a huge concern for my friend also who was working with me. Riya was their only daughter. Both her parents were working. Because it started affecting my friend's job, I thought of having a chat with Riya.

One Saturday I called her to the office. Riya came along with her father. I took her to a coffee shop nearby. It was only me and Riya. At the beginning of the discussion only, I told her that I would just try to help her overcome her anxiety. But the condition was that she has to tell me everything that happened from the 8th standard onwards. During the discussion, I realized that in her 8th standard, she had couple of new friends, who were trying to tease her that she wouldn't get the first grade in 8th standard. She started thinking too much on this. Every now and then she was only thinking about losing her first grade. Whenever she tried to concentrate on her studies she failed miserably as she was only worried about the first grade. This affected her concentration. She couldn't grasp things despite being a very studious girl. When the first term results came, she had already slipped to the second grade. This affected her confidence level badly. This kept on happening. So from a grade one student, she became an ordinary student. This is what anxiety can do to you!!

I understood her problem. I realised that it can be addressed easily. I realised, this could have been done by her parents if they would have bothered to chat with her openly. I spoke to Riya for couple of hours. I explained her entire issue of overthinking and getting anxious. I made her understand that she is not able to concentrate on studies because she is thinking too much about it. I asked her, what would happen if she lose, if she is not getting first grade. The only answer she had was, "my parents would shout at me". This poor girl was not even aware about a career that she would get if scores grade 1. That is the innocence these kid have !!!. I tackled it with a very silly point. I told her that now you are just an ordinary student. Hereon, you have got nothing to lose. I advised her to stop thinking about the 1st grade and focus on studying. Riya scored first grade in the 9th standard final exams.

This should be a learning for both parents and kids. Please don't over-stress on the grades. Focus on the process of learning. That is the best thing that you can do to your kid as a parent. Kids, if you face any problem you should openly interact with your parents. Don't be afraid of discussing anything with your parents. Parents are supposed to be your first friends. It is ok even if you don't get first grade. It is ok even if your parents are shouting at you because you are not first in the class or school. You will still be successful in your life. So chill and enjoy your studies don't be a victim of stress.

CHAPTER

Two

Negative Situations and Suicide

I was just twelve, when I came to know that one of my uncle committed suicide. It came as a shock to me. He had immense love for me. He always used to bring chocolates for me. I was shocked. That was my first exposure towards something called suicide. Later, I realised that my uncle was in debt and he had no money to repay. I still didn't understand as a kid, how committing suicide can repay his debts!!! I remember asking this to my mom and even she had no answer. After that I have lost good number of friends and relatives because of their suicides. While I was in my 10th standard, I lost one of my close friends. He committed suicide as a girl denied his proposal to be his girlfriend. I know it's often difficult to imagine what led a friend, family member, or celebrity to commit suicide. They give you no warning signs. You feel like what clues you might have missed. You wonder, whether you could have stopped them. You wonder committing suicide actually solved their problems or created more for the ones who are left behind. Let me tell you, many factors combine to lead to a decision to commit suicide. It is always an act made during a storm of strong emotions. Suicide is always committed when one really feels that there is no hope of survival.

Friends, what I have understood is that depression is one of the major reasons for suicide. Depression affects everyone but strong minded people survive. Since teenage is an age, where a kid is evolving as a strong human, teenagers are the most affected people. Hence, I would say suicide mentality is very common in teenagers, now a days. This is the age where parents have to be their kids' best friends. If the parents can be their best friends during this period to handhold them, these kids can be moulded as strong minded humans as they grow up. I have also come across adults who had the suicidal mentality. Time and again they keep threatening about committing suicide. It is nothing but a mental illness. In my man management career, I have seen many people who had suicidal tendencies. I have also come across strong people who thought about suicide at least once. I understood their reason was logical many a times. They felt it is all over for them. They didn't have the optimism to fight it out and hence they thought of committing suicide. Later, they agreed that it was the most foolish thought they ever had. Many of them were even ashamed that they thought about suicide. Giving up your life is never a solution to your problems. One should understand that very clearly.

Friends, as per my words of wisdom, only cowards commit suicide. This is what my parents have taught me. However, since I am talking about the suicide and situations leading to suicide, I would like to highlight certain common reasons that lead to suicide.

One may decide to commit suicide when he is sure that he has lost something and wouldn't be possible to regain it. This kind of situations can be as follows:

- Losing a relationship, especially love. This is very common reason for suicide.

- Another common reason is, when one loses money in business or loses a job. I have seen couple of instances wherein my friends have committed suicide after being sacked from the job.

- Too much of financial problems are often led to suicide. I mentioned about my uncle.

- Lot of students have committed suicide due to their failure in getting good grades.

- Lot of students have committed suicide due to the harassment in schools and colleges.

Reasons of committing suicide may vary. However, the core reason for the suicide is that, the suicider thought the situation can't be revived. He or she can't come out of it. Once they feel that it is really hopeless to live, they end their lives through suicide. This typically happens when you are unable to see whether a situation can be revived or not. They are too depressed that they become blind about the good things that can happen in their lives. They also don't realise that once they end their life, the problem due to which they commit suicide can affect their families. They are also unable to see the legal troubles their loved ones may have to go through. They forget that, if ending life would have been a solution to all the problems in this world, then there wouldn't have been any problems in life, rather there wouldn't have been any humans left as everyone is going through some or the other problem.

In this chapter, I would like to tell my readers why you shouldn't commit suicide however bad the situation you think is. You need to understand that nothing is permanent. Here I would like to tell you a small story of the Great Akbar and Birbal. Once Akbar called his minister Birbal and took him to a plain wall. He gave him a chalk and told him, write a statement on the wall in such a way that person who is happy becomes sad and vice versa after reading. Birbal wrote, **"Ye Waqt Gujar Jayega"**, means this time will pass. If you start thinking this in depth, you will fall in love with the wisdom of Birbal for which he is famous for. However difficult the situation is, time will change.

I have interacted with many people who had the suicidal thoughts. I had been successful in counselling them and was able to change their mind. People with suicidal thoughts need to understand few things clearly and keep telling them about this. However big is your pain in this world, you are not alone. Many of the successful personalities have gone through the pain which you are going through currently. They have overcome this phase and you too can do it. Many others are also in hopeless situation like you but they are not thinking about ending their life like you. Why should you do it? Why would you do it? What would happen to someone who loved you madly? However worse is your situation, there are people who loves you, people who need you. There are places where you can make a difference and excel. Remember that, life is all about facing problems bravely and not running away from it. You ending your life, may not be a solution at all.

One of the easiest ways to overcome this mind-set is to tell yourself that this time will change. Your emotions are not permanent. They keep changing. Emotions are always linked to situations. One of the classic example is, the same crowd you dislike in a bus, you embrace them in a club. Imagine how your loved ones would miss you, if you end your life!!! Irrespective of how bad things are, the creator, the God, the nature has the power to give you many things that you may want in life !!!. How would you enjoy them if you end your life?? So many good things may happen later on in your life and you have to be optimistic about this always. Every day brings you a new opportunity.

For all those who feel like committing suicide, there are few things that can change their mind and influence them positively.

1. You should constantly interact with someone. I have seen people who don't trust humans but they have made a really good connect with their pets. They have found hobbies to avoid depression. Positive people bring positivity to your life. I am of a firm believer that positivity attracts positivity and negativity attracts negativity. If you keep yourself involved with positive people, it can change your life positively.

2. You should consult a doctor who can advise you professionally. A proper consultation would have a huge impact on your mind. By doing this you are preparing a safety net for yourself.

3. You should lead a disciplined life, if possible with a written schedule for yourself. You should stick to it every day. Follow it religiously, even if you don't feel like.

4. Interacting with nature is another way. Expose yourself to nature. Go out on trekking. Play the games you like.

5. Doing daily exercise will not only help to build a strong body but help you to develop a strong mind. You may walk for just 30 minutes but follow it religiously. If 30 minutes is not possible start with 10 minutes and increase gradually.

6. Critical step would be to involve yourself in things that give you happiness. Some people find joy in pursuing their hobbies like music, dance etc. Some people find their happiness in travel. Do whatever you want but keep yourself involved and happy.

Above are the things that you should do. However, there are certain things that you should avoid strictly.

1. For people with suicidal mentality, I advise them to strictly avoid being alone. You should always be with someone. If that someone can be people whom you like and understand, that is much better.

2. You should always keep yourself from any sort of alcohol or drugs. This provokes negativity in your mind and always lead you to too many thoughts. Negative thoughts may lead to depression and provoke your suicidal thoughts.

3. Keep yourself away from negative people and negative circumstances as they can influence your mind easily. Keep yourself occupied. Reading is another thing which you can adapt. I have seen people improving their life after reading good books. Some people also depend on devotional side, trusting the lord almighty. You can try out that too.

In my own experience, I have seen teenagers (Students) committing suicide the most. I have always wondered why these guys commit suicide!!! And here lies my answer, expectation management. These kids are not matured enough to understand and set expectations for themselves. I would say, this is where your role as a parent comes into picture. If you can have open communication with your kids, understand their problems, your kids won't commit suicide. They will never be under stress. You should also make them understand that, everyone is not made for everything. The balance between sports and academics is essential for students. Someone may be good at studies and someone may be good at sports, this is how life is !!!. If your kids are able to absorb this during their childhood itself, life would be very easy for them. You would concrete them as better humans, who have the capability of facing anything and everything in life however bad it is.

I would quickly take another example from my own life. While I was a teenage student, I had a friend of mine Abhay. Abhay was always ahead of me in studies. However, he was never happy. We all friends used to tease him and used to ask him, what he wanted from life. He was always under tremendous pressure from his parents to be the number one student in the class. I recollect he was never happy with 99% also. I must admit that he was a scholar. He passed 12th with distinction. As he took admission in engineering, studies became his major concern. Post his first year results, he tried to commit suicide. However, his parents saved him. When I came to know about this, I called him up and spoke to him regarding the reason for his suicide attempt. He said, Rajesh I could not be first in the class. As a teenager, for me it was a very silly thing.

I decided to meet Abhay in person. I was very active in cricket those days. I won't shy away from saying that I was mad for cricket. I remember, I had left my maths paper half-done of the 12th final exam for a cricket tournament. When I met Abhay, I felt that he is completely a new person. I found him more sensible. Maybe he found his death in front of his eyes. He was very inquisitive about my cricket. We never spoke about his suicidal experience. Having said that, Abhay could not complete his engineering.

He said he didn't want to study engineering further, as he was not enjoying it. He finished his graduation in some other stream and today he works with a MNC as a Business Head. He is happily married. We don't speak often nowadays. Whenever we speak, we talk about our childhood and the golden days of our life. I recollect he telling me, post his 1st year Engineering exam, he thought he had lost everything and he didn't want to live. Today you look at him; he is happily married and successful. This is what time does to you. Have patience, don't think it is over, even if you feel it is over, you can still come back and make it big in your life.

You would always come across many situations where in you would feel that it is all over. I would like you to really look at the cover page of this book. A plant which was completely damaged during the construction of a concrete road, gave it's seed on the road. The seed had no opportunity to grow due to the lack of mud. However, it had the capability to fight back with the nature and give flower. Similar is your life, you can always have a beginning at any point of time. Always keep telling you **"Ye Waqt Gujar Jayega"**. Keep telling that nothing is permanent in life. Everything in life is temporary. If things are going good, enjoy it, because it won't last forever. If things are going bad, don't worry, it can't last forever either. Why worry and waste your life? Why take away your life which God has given you for which you have no right? Keep telling yourself **"Ye Waqt Gujar Jayega"** and a new ray of hope emerges in your mind. It gives you power, it gives you wisdom to think. So remember, the mantra is **"Ye Waqt Gujar Jayega"**.

CHAPTER
Three

Depression and Relationships

My dear readers, what I am going to write here, most of you would have gone through. It would be very silly to ask how many of you have fallen in love? At some point or other, we all must have fallen in love. Relationships are a very crucial aspect of our life. Most of us take it very seriously. You might have read a lot of news that celebrities are in depression, especially after their breakup. Many a times I read it and I felt surprised. I always thought why someone should fight depression, especially in case of a breakup? Over the years, I have realised that it is a matter of setting your expectations right. Depression comes because of your poor expectation management. When I say this like a Guru, I understand that it is not easy for everyone. Managing expectation is really an art. It is not everybody's cup of tea. Through this chapter, I would like to address this concern of overcoming your depression through proper expectation management. Expectations leads to disappointment; disappointment leads to depression. You are in the middle of a sea where you do not know what to do next. Throughout this book, I would only talk about how to overcome depression, negativities and problems so that you can set your life in the right direction.

Many times you might have heard people saying that, trust is the base of any relationship. I would like to add one more important factor to the success of any relationship and that is clear communication. Relationship fails miserably in the absence of clear communication and trust. However deeper is the relationship, without both the above factors, it can't survive. I wouldn't say that only these factors affect the relationship. If you look at your own lives, you will realise that many relationships struggle due to the ego. Whether it is love or friendship, whenever it is affected by ego, it suffers or ends. When the relationship ends, it leads to depression. It leads to committing suicide. Some people replace it with drugs and alcohol. There is no need to end a relationship if mutual respect is given along with clear communication. In my life, I have seen divorces happening as there is a lack of clear communication. Ego comes in between the husband-wife and then they separate. This can be avoided and they can live a happy life. Through this chapter, I want to express my views towards having a strong relationship.

Let me give you two different perspectives of looking at relationships and depression. On one side, I would like to look at people like me, who are happily married and on the other side, I would like to look at people who often change relationship status. Let me take this example of myself, I and my wife met 20 years ago. Initially, we were in love, then when we decided to live together. We opted for a live-in for 2 years and finally got married in 2006. The day when we started living together, we had set expectations for ourselves. We agreed on the do's and don'ts in our relationship. I never meant to say that we are a perfect couple. However, I find our relationship much better than other relationships. Maybe you would also feel the same for others if you have a successful relationship with your partner. I would say that, the success of our relationship is purely due to the expectation management set between us. When you are expecting certain things and it doesn't happen, it leads to depression. The most critical thing in a relationship is clear communication. If there is proper and clear communication, half of the problems are already addressed there, rather I would say that it won't exist. Most of the times, people get possessive about their relationships. This possessiveness knowingly or unknowingly set expectation standards within their minds. And then, when things don't work out, it leads to disappointment further piling up on the depression. Many of my friends ask me, how am I able to manage a healthy work-life balance. Especially those people who know me very closely and they know how workaholic I am. To them my initial answer is the expectation that my wife has from me. I know you are confused let me clarify.

Since we have been together for a very long time, we know each other much better than anyone else, including our parents. This obviously has made our lives very easy. I know what she likes and she knows what I want. I know for a fact that this is not a very regular case with most of the readers here. But it is not a herculean task to know your partner and set expectations very very clearly. However, workaholic you are, however busy you are making money or however struggling you are, it is very important to give time to your family. Healthy work-life balance can only improve things in your life. One most important thing which you need to understand in a relationship is that, you are not supposed to know anything and everything in life. I and my wife practice this very regularly in our day to day life. I am strongly of the opinion that you are only supposed to know things which are in your control. There is no point in knowing things which are not in your control, as it only consumes your mind. This is a very common thing between me and my wife wherein we tell each other only those things which are relevant. To give you an example, in my daily life, I go through so many problems related to my business. Out of this, there are certain problems for which my wife may have a solution. Despite her being a promoter of our company, I would only discuss those problems which are there in her control and she would be able to give me a solution. By doing so, as a partner I am seeking her valuable inputs to my problems. At the same time, I am also ensuring that I am not cascading anything which is not there in her control and putting unnecessary stress on her. This increases mutual respect and also ensures that you are not consuming your partner's mind. This leads to a healthy and peaceful lifestyle.

Like I mentioned earlier many times, I have always wondered why people get into depression when their relationship fails. I am not only talking about a common man but I am also talking about people who are at higher levels. Whether they are a CEO of a company or they are a big celebrity, they also get depression when their relationship fails. If the relationship is so critical for them, why don't they respect it initially when the relationship existed? I remember reading an article about one of the leading Bollywood actress who went into depression after her relationship failed. I was shocked. I always perceived her as a brave woman. She was in love with one of the emerging Bollywood male stars, their relationship was very open, everybody knew about it. Later on, in the article she claimed that he dumped her. She went into so much of depression that her career got stalled. She had to consult a psychiatrist. She was out of the industry for almost two years. I must say that, everybody wrote her off completely. In an interview, she said that she even thought of committing suicide. She was in mad love with him. She felt that she has been used and this led to depression. To her luck, with the help of the psychiatrist, she could come out of the depression in 2 years' time. She clearly said that, it was the worst period of her life, especially after seeing success in the initial days of her career.

I also read couple of articles on her boyfriend's views. I was curious to know, what led to the breakup of their relationship. He also had the similar views. He said that he has been used by her so that she could become popular. He said he has been dumped after she got success. He said she had multiple affairs at the same time. If you consider both the parties as genuine, you would agree that, it was a matter of expectation management. Maybe, both of them loved each other very madly and very deeply. The deep love led to a natural possessiveness. Possessiveness created expectations. When expectations were not met, it went into disappointment and doubts. That led to the breakup and since they were were genuinely in love, the person with the weaker heart went into depression. Because the guy had a stronger heart, may be it didn't affect him that much. He had the guts to overcome that phase. And like I said in the earlier chapters, he must have told himself **"Ye Waqt Gujar Jayega"**.

The girl today, after overcoming her depression, is Bollywood's number 1 actress. She is admired as the most successful married female actor. But have you ever imagined how those two years would have been for her in depression? She might have gone through a hell !!! Enough videos are available on YouTube which will help you understand how to overcome depression, after the failure of a relationship. Most of these experiences would only talk to you regarding the expectation management that you should have in a relationship. After fighting the depression, she again fell in love with a boy to whom she got married. Today this couple is admired as the most successful couple in Bollywood. She also wanted to commit suicide during her depression period. She also felt, it is all over for her. However, she decided to fight it out, she overcame that period and now you can see how successful she is! Imagine if she would have quit at that point of time while she was in depression!! Do you think she would have been able to see this day? This is what I wanted to say time and again, never ever quit. It is just a matter of time which is bad and not you. Keep telling yourself that, if you quit now, you won't be able to succeed. Keep telling yourself that **"Ye Waqt Gujar Jayega"**. Nobody's going to tell it for you, only you and you are responsible for this. It is your life and it is in your hands.

Another philosophy that I want to tell you from my own experience that, how true is your love !!! The concept of true love have been twisted many times. Some people say that only mothers have the true love. As an individual, it is your choice what you want to enjoy. I keep telling my wife that it's ok even if you do not love me truly, but be expressive that you love me. What is the use of that true love which I cannot enjoy today? Rather I prefer to have love which is expressive and can be felt. If you recollected your own initial days of affair, you would agree that there had been less of possessiveness and more of care. This created a mutual respect. However, as the days passed, things started to become regular and normal in the relationship. You felt that you are made for each other. The mutual admiration and the respect that you had for each other had become a command then. That command led to possessiveness. By the time you got married, or your relationship got older, your expectations also went high. This is the reason why most of the love marriages fail.

To summarise this chapter, I would say that, have your expectations set right in the relationship. Don't go overboard. Consider everyday as a new day and new beginning of the relationship. Imagine every morning that you are meeting or interacting with a new person. If at all you had a very bad day in relationship, that's not the end of relationship. Even if you broke up, that is not the end of your life. You may get someone better than what you had. Don't lose hope. There is still a tomorrow. Every day brings you a new hope, new experience. The only thing is you have to be mentally ready for that. So don't get depressed if you lose a relationship, God has made something, someone better for you. Wait for it; live in your hope positively than giving up.

CHAPTER *Four*

Self Esteem, Ego and Career

Readers how many of you feel that you have a very high ego? How many of you have ever done something and then regretted about it? How many of you feel that such kind of an act has caused you a big damage? Since my childhood, I have always been an egoistic person. I always kept my self-esteem high. However, I have learnt that there is a very thin line between self-esteem and ego. This, I learnt from my own experiences. I won't shy away from saying that, I learnt it after the big losses that I have made in my own life because of the ego. I was very blessed that I learnt about these things at a very young age. My ego had made me face losses as a student; my ego had made me face losses at the initial stage of my career and because of my ego, I had lost good friends but all these things happened at a very younger age. By the time I was 25, I had already learnt all these things from my own experiences. I have had so many friends and colleagues who had lost good opportunities because of their ego. Why does your ego come in between you and your work? Have you ever thought about it? Have you ever sat down and anticipated how things would have been without your ego? Your ego is nothing but a luggage that you carry on your back and in your brain. This makes you very uncomfortable. This makes you unproductive. This makes you useless.

Imagine a scenario where in your brain is open, your mind is open, you are able to receive things as it comes to you without any filtration, without any prejudice. You would be able to see it in a very different perspective. Things would be much clearer to you without the filter. Filter is nothing but your ego. If I have to put it in other words, I would say that you are not receiving things as it comes to you because of the filtration that you are putting in between. Your ego creates a big communication gap in terms of understanding between you and the person in front of you. I have had the opportunity to work with multi-talented people in the last 15 years. Some of them were really excellent. Today as I see, they have been eradicated from the system because of their ego. Have you ever thought why this filtration comes in between? Here also, I must say that expectation management plays a vital role in receiving things as it comes to you in its natural form. Your ego is like a blindness; you are not able to see a real picture leading to incorrect perceiving of a thing. This creates a severe dent in your life and in career as well. Think and think about this. You will be able to understand what I am saying. You will be able to read my mind. Ego ruins everything in your life and pulls you down from big heights and that fall is so severe that you would take ages to recover.

Many egoistic people, whom I know, claim that, it is not their ego but self-esteem. Like I mentioned earlier there is a very thin line between the ego and self-esteem. People, who are able to understand it, differentiate it well. Many times, I have wondered why somebody has so much of ego? How life would have been different for them if they would have not had this ego. As a child, my parents gave me everything that I wanted. They never stopped me from doing anything that I wanted to do. I must say that this created a lot of over-confidence in me. This overconfidence gradually developed as my ego and it had started reflecting in anything and everything that I did. Initially I did not understand this. I was unable to judge the damage this could do. Our ego puts a kind of shadow in our mind; we are unable to see what we are doing and what we are talking. I will go one step ahead and say that, it would also put a shadow in our brain because of which we are unable to take correct decisions. Our ego makes us overconfident that we start underestimating the people in front of us. We feel that we are really big and the people in front of us are very small. Your ego also can be arrested with the set of expectation management procedures. Your ego will completely arrest your learning skills. You are not at all receptive. You refuse to agree that you are wrong or you may be wrong.

Despite saying so many things, some people still argue that self-esteem and the ego are the same. In our childhood, we were always taught to be not selfish. We were always taught to help others. I have seen many people who have been labelled as egoistic and selfish, but when I became close to them and understood them well, I realised that those views are wrong. Hence it is also important to talk about perception management. The entire world runs on this concept. In the coming days, I may write one entire book on perception management. Most of the times, people perceive one as egoistic or selfish. They may appear so due to their external behaviour. At the bottom of their heart they may not be egoistic or selfish. Hence before you label someone as egoistic or selfish, let us try to understand certain differences between self-esteem and ego.

1. Love and Admiration for Oneself

I find this as a common feature of egoist people. They love themselves too much. Their admiration for self goes to a level wherein they refuse to see the reality. Another big problem with these kinds of people is that they think they are better than other people. According to them, they are perfect and everyone else is imperfect. They feel and decide that only they can do things perfectly and others always goof-up. There is a very thin line between self-esteem and ego. So people with high self-esteem also value themselves high but they don't consider others low. They don't think that others are imperfect. They don't think only they can do anything correctly. This is their best quality and differentiates themselves from egoistic people. People with high self-admiration also accept the reality that nobody is perfect. They don't downgrade anyone. They help others to overcome their deficiencies. They don't pull anybody's morale down. Hence, you should be able differentiate yourself, what are you, an egoistic person or a person with high self-esteem??

2. Selfishness

Selfishness is a common factor in egoistic people. They love themselves and are least bothered about others. The always want to be the center of attraction. If they are ignored, they react angrily. They get disappointed fast. However, people with healthy self-esteem think about themselves but they also think about others. They are genuinely concerned about others. They are good listeners and they show sympathy. It is never wrong to have high self-esteem. I am one of those who carry myself with high self-esteem. However, it is completely wrong to think that others are inferior to me.

Einstein said, "You cut and style your hair, but you always forget to do the same with your ego".

3. Beyond the Beliefs

I have always found that people with high ego carry certain thoughts and beliefs in their mind. Either they have been taught or they must have adapted from somewhere. Most of the times, they refuse to go beyond their beliefs. They think that their perspective is correct and other's is completely wrong. Egoistic people never like to be questioned on their beliefs. In fact, they can't digest the fact that they are being questioned. This is nothing but a blindness that digs their grave. On the other side, people with self-esteem are easy to be approached. They accept their faults and try to improve always. They are also open to new ideas. This helps them learn and grow, while egoistic people die their natural death with their ego.

4. Can't Accept Criticism

Egoistic people can't hear anything negative about them. They always love to hear good flattering things about themselves. If they find anyone questioning them or criticising them, they lose their cool. This is the biggest problem with egoistic people. They take it as a personal attack on themselves instead of understanding the value of the criticism. Hence you may note that, people with ego fails miserably time and again. They get angry and blame other people time and again. On the other hand, those with healthy self-esteem are able to recognize their defects and accept it. They use criticism for their change and use it to become better people. They won't take criticism as being negative. Rather, they appreciate it when it's constructive.

5. Always Expect Return Gifts

Egoistic people are also selfish most of the time and they won't do anything free of cost for anyone. They always expect something or the other, which I call return gift. They can't see someone prospering and doing well in life. They will always try to do damage because of this. If they are looking for help or seem interested in something, it's because they stand to benefit in some way or the other. On the other hand, people with good self-esteem never do this. They always try to help people selflessly. They are least affected by someone's progress. They take it as a positive learning and implement good things in their life.

6. Others are Inferior

If you notice the biggest difference between selfish people and people with healthy self-esteem. People with big ego think that they are above everyone else. They always admire themselves as the best. They always believe that others can't do what they can do. People with self-esteem seldom think that all are equal. They try to learn from people who are better than them. They speak the truth most of the times and advise people who are weaker than them. They don't make comparisons.

From the above points try and analyse yourself. In which category do you fall? This will help you to be a better person, a person with self-esteem and not ego. I agree that at some point or the other all of us must have acted selfishly and many a times in future we will. All I am trying to say is to not let your ego come in between you and things. You miss the opportunity of seeing real things. You would be able to get respect and love. You would be able to see things in a different perspective. It is also to be noted that you would be able to live a better life when you become selfless and start giving. Giving is always a pleasure. Many Saints have said this and now I am personally experiencing it. There is a huge pleasure in giving. You always get back whatever you have given. People with healthy self-esteem respect, accept, value and love themselves. As a result, they are able to have satisfying, fruitful relationships. They aren't selfish; they're learning what they need so they then can provide it to others.

Now what do you think?? You have ego or self-esteem? What makes you feel insecure? Why do you want people to pay attention to you? Think about it. You can't have a big ego and healthy self-esteem at the same time.

I remember a guy, who is very aggressive while talking. Most of the people who interacted with him have stamped him as an egoistic person. In the initial days of interactions, I also felt the same. However, I got to know him over a period of time. One day, I asked him, why he carries so much of ego. He said, Rajesh I am not egoistic but I can't listen to anyone. I don't need to listen to anyone. This is my self-esteem and self-respect. I closely observed his actions and I realised that he has a misunderstanding between self-esteem and ego like most of the egoistic people. I made him understand the art of listening openly without any prejudice. I explained him how life would be simple for him. I explained that he can get rid of his blood pressure issue by this simple method. I also advised him to meditate. I happen to meet him again after 2 years. He was a completely different man. He was much fitter after losing a lot of weight. He thanked me and said that he has stopped taking the medicines for blood pressure. He was reborn, I would say with a smile on my face.

To all those people who say that, I do not have ego and it's my self-esteem, this chapter would help them dramatically change their mind set. They would agree that, they have been completely wrong. They could have had a better perspective towards looking at things and hearing things. This would have made their life simpler. This would have made them a better person. Probably this would have made them more successful. Irrespective of that, this would definitely help them climb-up the ladder. So kill your ego, open your mind and brain, this will help you succeed in life. It is not about success but the happiness that you get when you are not putting your ego in between anything.

CHAPTER
Five

Fear of Being You

How many of you hold yourself back due to the fear of rejection? Many of us want to do a lot of things in life but we are not able to do it because of the fear that we have in our mind, the fear of being ourselves. I have come across many people who are afraid of expressing themselves. I have noticed this when I have told people to speak few words about themselves. I have seen this in the interviews that I have taken. I have seen this in the students whom I have taught. There is always a fear of being you. I have wondered why this happens!!! Is it due to the fear of rejection? Is it due to the fear of failure? I think both. I have seen people with experience also having this problem. They fail to express themselves. It is a very ridiculous thing but that's how life is !!

I had a colleague of mine, he was my junior and he carried himself very well. He had a very nice personality. I found his IQ level very high. He was very good at his work. I wanted to promote him to the next level because of the good work that he has done. However, I was very concerned about his stage-fear. This came as a concern from my Senior also when I recommended him for a promotion. I was clueless what to do. I called for a meeting with him. I told him about this. He was very nervous. He started sweating. Maybe he was afraid of losing his promotion. I decided to agree on terms with him. I told him that, if he can overcome his stage fear, he can easily get promoted. I said initially he has to address a group of 5 unknown people. He agreed. But as the time neared, he started losing his confidence. He came to me and told me that he cannot do it. I tried to pacify him that he can do it. I convinced him that he should give it a try at least. I told him that I would be there to support him. We went to the stage. He was shivering. He looked at me helplessly. I motivated him. He went on to the stage and addressed the crowd. Initial few seconds he was lacking confidence. But he held on to it. He could speak for 10 minutes on the agenda we had agreed. He did it nicely. We both were very proud of what he has done. I said we should try more sessions and he gladly agreed. Later on he became a Training Manager. Now he takes motivational sessions for all..... To all those who are afraid of expressing themselves, please take a lesson out of this. It is a matter of beginning and then you are through.

Do you know that your greatest joy and satisfaction comes when you are being real? When you are unable to express yourself you are always in a shell. What stops you from being you? What do you think is lacking in you because of which you cannot be yourself? Ironically it is the biggest pain not giving to life and to others according to your potential. God has created you with something or the other. You are unique in your own way. Don't think that you are inferior to someone. The real potential of whatever you are can really be exhibited if you behave yourself as You. I have had interaction with many people whom I asked about this fear. Surprisingly most of them didn't have an answer !! Some people are introvert because from childhood they have been facing bashes. They have been always told that they are not good at things. If you are one amongst them, my question to you, who are those people to judge you? Who are they to say that you are not good at something? Nobody has the right to judge anyone. I cannot tell you that you are good or bad something. I neither have the power, nor have the right. So don't feel that somebody has judged you and you are incapable. There is something special in you and you are the one who can identify that and act on it. You can be excellent in that. So go ahead and discover what you are good at, your life will change, you will overcome all the fears, you will be happy. Most importantly, you will be able to do excellent in whatever you are doing as you're doing it without any fear.

One can end the fear only through self-alienation. Otherwise, it takes away your happiness. Since the inner processes become inverted, you lose contact with your innermost being. The biggest concern out of all this is that you are not able to listen to your mind, you want to do it but still you are unable to do it. You are in a mess. You are unreal and underperforming on your potential. The only way to come out of this is to be the real you. When you are not presenting yourself to others, they are judging someone else in your form. This may have consequences in your life. You pretend to be something but people see you as the same person you are pretending. There is no need to be unreal. The moment you open up yourself, you will enjoy the freedom, you will see a new world. Many big personalities have gone through this phase once. So you are not different. Unleash the real you and world would be different for you.

For your better conviction, let me talk about the story of a Bollywood star. He was born to one of the biggest Bollywood director. He had everything since his childhood barring confidence. He could not speak fluently because of his stammering. Being inspired by his dad, he always wanted to be an actor. However, he was sceptical to even tell this to his father. He was sent to the best of the universities for his higher studies, he had no interest in that. He went because his dad wanted him to go. Somehow, he managed to complete his studies. He then started assisting his father in his direction work. One fine day, his father came to know that, his son wanted to be an actor. When he asked his son, why he didn't tell it earlier, he said he was afraid of stammering. He said he doubted whether he could deliver dialogues. His father was a wise man. He immediately sent him for a speech therapy; he started the preparation for his first movie. However, his son was not confident. He insisted that his son act in the movie. Over the next few months he could convince his son that he can be an actor. Son started getting results from the speech therapy that he attended. He could speak much fluently without stammering. The father never gave up, he persuaded him, kept motivating him always. Somehow they completed the movie.

The movie was the biggest hit of that year. The actor went on to get so many accolades like Best Actor, Best newcomer etc. During one of the interview, the actor disclosed these things. He gave a fantastic speech during the award ceremony. Nobody would have even recognised that he had a stammering problem. Today, he is an international icon; he is admired as the most handsome man in Asia and top five in the world. This is the power, if you unleash your real you. This is the difference it can bring to your life. The actor's friends who used to tease him once are not visible anywhere. Nobody knows them. Maybe today, they are also a fan of this actor. This is how life plays with you when you are real. When you don't give up and are ready to face any challenges life throws at you. Everyone who once said bad about you, will become your admirer and will praise you. They will tell the world that they know you. Hence, tear off the mask, get out of the shell and look at your potential. There is something big awaiting you.

To summarise, I would say that there are enough capabilities within you which stops once you are indulged in not being you. The real potential of you the way god has created you is only fruitful when you are natural. So go ahead and be the real you. The creator has given you something unique which he hasn't given to anyone else. Only you can unveil the real you. I always believed in the statement, one can only take the horse to the water, drinking has to be done by the horse. Same is the case with you being you. People can tell you various methods and give you plenty of ideas, however you have to practice and ensure that you are not exhibiting an artificial version of you anywhere. With so many people, you don't *need* to be accepted by everyone. You don't even need to be accepted by *most* people. There are only a few people who you will genuinely get along with or enjoy spending your time with…so why settle? This is getting dangerously close to the advice I hate most for socially anxious people, "stop worrying what other people think." Of course it would be great if you could do that, but it's not that easy. Instead of trying to get everyone to like you, try to think about whether you are really compatible with *them*. This shifts your mind-set away from a fear of rejection to finding out what they can offer you. And if they reject you…chances are that they weren't a good fit in the first place. You don't have to be perfect every time you do something. In other words, you can do everything "right" and still be rejected. So instead of thinking of rejection as "failure," attach success to the act of *trying*.

CHAPTER
Six

*Master the Art of Not
Giving-Up*

Ever since, I learnt the art of not giving-up, I wanted to tell the world about it. While I was learning about this at the age of 24-25, one person who influenced me significantly is M.S Dhoni. I recalled the 2007, first T 20 World Cup final. Everyone had lost hopes about India's win. However, we got surprised by the thought process of our captain M.S Dhoni. Since then I have been his great fan. Several times he has got India out of mess in the last over. The art of not giving-up is my favourite subject. I can speak for hours and hours on this.

It is quite natural that we all become discouraged. Before you close on something you've been working toward, remember that every difficulty is an opportunity in disguise. The most successful people in the world have always failed multiple times. We know that K. Rowling, Walt Disney, Albert Einstein, Vincent van Gogh, Thomas Edison, and Dr. Seuss have one thing in common and that is they failed multiple times. I remember the quote from Edison, "I have not failed. I've just found 10,000 ways that won't work. I am not discouraged because every wrong attempt discarded is another step forward". Einstein didn't speak until he was 4 and didn't read until he was 7, after which he went on to win the Nobel Prize and became the face of modern physics. Van Gogh only sold one painting in his lifetime, and that was to a friend. Even so, he kept painting and finished more than 800 pieces. His most expensive painting today is valued at $142.7 million. J. K. Rowling was famously rejected by 12 publishers before *Harry Potter and the Philosopher's Stone* was accepted. Walt Disney, according to legend, was turned down 302 times before he got financing for creating Disneyland. So before you think of quitting, think again, why you started it. Than looking at how much is left, look at how far you have travelled and how much pain you have already taken in process. Let me tell you readers, I strictly am against quitting on anything that I want. I have learnt that if I don't quit, one day I will succeed. Here also I apply the same philosophy of **"Ye Waqt Gujar Jayega"**. I want you also to learn and believe in this mantra and see the magic.

Whenever I am tired of not getting result on something that I have been working hard, here's what I try to remind myself of when I feel like giving up…

My Mind will Change

I know that at this juncture my mind wants something and it will change later. So you have to consider every thought you have as a suggestion, not an order. Right now my mind is suggesting something and after sometime my mind will suggest something else. If I am able to understand this, if I am able to pass that period, I will definitely not quit. I didn't start it to quit, I started to become successful. This is what I have to tell my mind, this is what I have to tell myself. If my mind is suggesting to give up right now, the same mind had asked me to start this. So, tomorrow again my mind may say that, I want to do it. Consider it as an option and move on. Don't quit your mind will change.

My Discomfort is not Permanent

I want to quit because I have been working on this and I have not been getting success. I have been able to see a discomfort in myself. However, I also need to understand that this discomfort is not permanent. This discomfort is temporary. If you overcome this particular discomfort, you may witness success. Your life may change. If you become a victim of this discomfort and quit, you will never be successful that's for sure.

You will be successful one day. We all want to be successful. We all want our work to be respected. We all want our body to be admired by others. Have you ever thought what are we doing to achieve all these? But have you ever thought, am I putting in the desired efforts? We all want the results but we are not ready to grind for it. When you feel like quitting, don't forget that, if you do not quit then you would be successful one day. Your success will have no complaints, you will have no complaints and nobody ever will have any complaints. That's the beauty of success. Keep telling this to yourself whenever you feel like quitting, I bet you won't quit. The world is such that everybody wants to be successful, but nobody is willing to work hard for it. You can be different if you don't quit.

Tell Yourself, there are Many Failures before Success

Life is a constant struggle. Everyone who has tasted success has gone through this space. The reason today they are successful is that they did not give up at the point of their struggle. They fought it over to become successful. You have to always overcome your distractions and pains to be successful. Whenever you feel like not doing something after starting it, hold on for a while, your mind may change, your feelings will change, you will again feel like starting it and success would touch your feet. Life is all about daily battles and decisions that you will have to take to survive. Keep telling this to yourself and you will never feel like quitting on something that you really wanted.

Over the years, I have practiced certain ideas that I learnt from many books and articles and training programs I attended and this has helped me become a non-quitter. I have tried to narrate the same here below for your benefit.

1. Why did you start it?

This is the beginning that you should keep reminding yourself. It will keep you motivated always and you would never feel to quit. This is nothing but the purpose with which you started.

2. Great things take time and efforts

Anything great is worth fighting for. Great things take time, but great things happen all at once.

3. My favourite, it's not over

I have seen many people who quit after making one attempt. Don't be that person. Do all you can to succeed, even when the entire world is against you? Even if it is your last breath, it is worth attempting. Nature would have a surprise for you. Keep telling yourself, it's not over yet, I'm still alive.

4. Get away from negative attitude

Always tell yourself that negative thoughts create negative results. Always throw away your negative thoughts with positive thoughts. Positivity attracts success.

5. Take responsibility

You can't always control the results. But you own your efforts, your ideas, and your perseverance against obstacles.

6. Learn from your mistakes

It is a universal truth that everyone makes mistakes. Nobody is perfect. No one has achieved anything without making mistakes. But you have to learn from the things that go wrong so that you can correct it in future. Next time you can be prepared enough to not repeat the same mistakes.

7. Nobody got success in the first attempt. Try multiple times

Nobody got success in the first attempt. Just because you didn't get it right the first time, that doesn't mean you won't get it right the second. It also means that even if you didn't succeed in the first five attempts, it doesn't mean that you won't succeed in the sixth attempt. So before you quit everything or give up on anything remember that, while you can never go back and have a new beginning, you can always start now and make a new ending.

There are many reasons why somebody quit. Some can be internal like from within themselves, some can be because we keep extending our decision and actions, some can be because we are being influenced by others and some can be due to situations. There may be other reasons also, broadly we can categorise them into the above four. When I say obstacle within us, I am talking about our mind. Our mind has the capability of influencing as badly. Many times we are blinded to this. One of the key obstacles is the fact that we don't have enough desire. It simply means that we want to have something but we are not willing to work for it. Since we are not willing to work for it, we don't get it and ultimately we end up quitting. I also feel that our self-belief plays a vital role in helping us achieve something that we desperately want. Many a time our self-belief also comes as a barrier as an obstacle in our success. If you do not have a firm belief in your abilities, your systems result from not having enough confidence and you fail. So you will lack the willpower to fight consistently and overcome the hurdles. Another thing which is missing in you, you want it but your desire and commitment is not strong. So you fail and then you quit.

Let me share another example of myself. I joined DBS Bank in the year 2010. Until then I had around 6 years of experience, but not in banking sector. I had been in insurance sector before I joined the bank. Before joining the bank, I had to clear several rounds of interview. Post joining the bank, I struggled a lot in the initial 6 months. Even my juniors were not willing to accept me. They thought that I knew nothing. They all had around 8 to 10 years of experience in banking. My lack of knowledge affected my operation style. It gave me poor results. There were days in 2011 when I almost thought of quitting the job. I somehow managed to regain my confidence. I asked myself about the purpose with which I joined the bank. Did I really join the bank to quit? Did I really join the bank to quit as a loser? Who are my juniors to tell me that I cannot do something or not? I decided to fight back. I started studying about processes, I started studying about products and I started studying about operations. Initially, it was really boring as it was very difficult. I didn't want to do it. Every time I thought of quitting, every time I thought of giving up, I reminded myself the purpose of joining the bank. I wanted to be successful. I wanted to be called as an Investment Banker. I started meeting more customers. Through my interaction with my customers, I gained more knowledge. I had to answer their queries, for that I had to prepare myself. As I entered in 2012, I lost most of my juniors because of their poor performance. They were asked to leave the bank. I survived, because I had a strong will to emerge as a performer. My boss must have seen that in me. Within 3 months of 2012, I emerged as the number two performer PAN India. I was able to salvage my lost Pride. I was always a performer wherever I worked. I didn't want to quit as a loser. This is the attitude that differentiates successful people and people who quit. Hence, I have titled this book the way it is. I have dedicated this book to those people who were once almost finished. They had the fire within themselves to fight back I am sure today they are successful.

Hope I have been able to give you a better clarity. Don't give up on your dreams. You have the power within you to accomplish it. Keep trying and you will succeed.

CHAPTER
Seven

Addictions and Life

Most of us are addicted to something or the other in our lives. However, addiction is perceived as a very bad word. When thinking of the term "addiction" many people associate it with drugs. Thinking of an "addict" often brings forth images of someone in the streets looking for their next fix of heroin or cocaine. While addiction to drugs is a common problem, the term "addiction" is not limited to only illicit street drugs. Some are addicted to tobacco, some are addicted to alcohol and some are addicted to their smartphones. I would say that addiction is just a state of mind. Weak minded people are not able to control their mind and hence they call themselves as addicts. How on Earth it is possible that your mind doesn't listen to you. Are you a slave of your mind? Or your mind is your slave? As a reader of this book what do you think what is your addiction? What is it that you are really addicted to? Why do you think so? I have come across many strong minded people who once thought that they are addicted to something or the other. I had a very close colleague of mine; he always consumed 2 packets of cigarettes in a day. Many a times we tried to convince him that it is very injurious to health. He kept saying that he can't live without it. He was professionally very successful. The way he consumed it, we were sure that one day he would collapse. However, to our surprise one fine day he told us that he is quitting cigarettes. We felt that he is joking. We were very sure that he would not be able to do it. To our surprise he did it. Initially for him it was a fight with his body than mind. However, later the story changed. When his body started adapting to it, it was a big fight with his own mind. In the initial seven days I realised his craving was killing him. However, he decided to fight it out. He was very determined that he would never touch it under whatever circumstances. Whenever I spoke to him I realised the determination that he had within himself. I admired how strong he was. It has been almost 5 years that he has not touched a cigarette after that. In the initial days, he could never stand along with a smoker. Now, he enjoys party with them. This is the power of mind. You should never be a slave of your mind. If you can make your mind your slave, I must say that you have arrived in life. Most of your problems would vanish if your mind is your slave. Practice it and see the magic.

Have you ever thought how can you get rid of your addictions? The good news is that you can quit, although it is a complicated process. There are many factors, physical, mental, and emotional, that make quitting difficult. This is why so many people find treatment helpful to guide them through the complex process of quitting – although many people are successful quitting on their own. Understanding why quitting is so difficult can help you see that everyone overcoming an addiction goes through the same process to some extent. It is not that you are especially weak-willed or that you are failing any more than anyone else.

When you find yourself thinking, feeling, or acting in a particular way that goes against your decision to quit, you can be more compassionate with yourself, and keep trying.

Let me also tell you another real life example. One of my friend, who was fully addicted to alcohol. He used to consume more than 540 ml daily. He was very young. He started drinking casually with friends and then it became a daily affair. Slowly, he got addicted. He lost everything that he had, including this job. This put him in more trouble as he started to borrow money and drink. Gradually people stopped giving him money. He couldn't bear even a minute in the evening without alcohol. He stared to behave like a mad man. Few of his friends forcefully took him to a de-addiction centre in Bangalore where he was admitted for almost 30 days. When he came out, he was a new man totally. I caught up with him post treatment to understand his experience. For an addict it was horrible in the initial 7 days. I remember that he wanted to end his life. The system out there in the de-addiction centre was very strong. They monitored their patients very closely because of which he couldn't end his life. Presently, he is working with a private firm and his wife and kids have come back into his life.

Most of the times, you may have started something casually and then over a period of time you must have got addicted to it. Something like a smoke or a drink. I had been to Macau 2013. I was staying at Hotel Venetian. It is considered as the hub of Casino in Macau. I generally don't play in Casino. I went with my friends to give them a company. They were playing and I was watching. They were playing roulette. On the same table I spotted an old lady. She might have been in her early seventies. She was playing really big games. Betting really big, we were astonished, how rich she might have been !! Slowly my friends started leaving. Most of them lost their money that they carried to the Casino. As I was not sleepy and as I was curious about this old lady, I decided to stay back. I observed her closely. Whenever, I felt like she is almost exhausted with her money, she would win the last round. I thought she is a part of the Casino; she has been placed there to influence the customers. At around four o'clock in the morning, she lost everything that she had. She packed her bags and started to leave. She looked at me and gave me a smile as I was sitting there for a long time. I shook hands with her and gave her my introduction. I asked her if she would like to join me for a drink. She gladly agreed.

We sat on a table and grabbed our drinks. I introduced myself. She told me that she was from China. Now settled in Macau. She said she could not live without playing Casino. Her kids were in the US. They sent her money every month. Once she visited Macau on a trip with her friends. They stayed in the same hotel. She was introduced to the Casino for the first time. She played for the first time and won the money. She wanted to play again. She played the next day and won again. Third day she lost everything that she had. She wanted to gain it back, at least the capital. She went to China, and came back to Macau again to play Casino. Again she lost everything that she had. She kept coming to Macau only to play Casino. The time that I had met her, she had shifted to Macau to play Casino. She realised that she got addicted to it. She didn't tell me how much money she had lost in Casino, but she said she lost more than what she earned. I asked her what if she stops playing. She said she cannot live without it. She has to play daily. This was the first time that I got to know about an addiction towards Casino. When I Googled it, I realised that there are many people like her. Most of them have only lost money. That's the addiction that they have.

Now let me also tell you a little bit of the social media addictions where people claim that they have so many friends and followers on Instagram and twitter. Is it really worth wasting time assuming those are real relationships? When you are with a real life person sharing a conversation, a meal, or a cup of coffee, they are a real life form. A real person right there in front of you to engage with. Are you telling me that your virtual friends and virtual text conversations are more important than the real life person in front of you? Not only is this the rudest thing on the planet, but it breaks down friendships and can ruin relationships. Even if you say to a friend "Oh I just need to check that," They may respond "Oh, that's ok." But the truth is it's not ok. What you are saying is that the virtual message is more important than them. They have taken time out of their busy life to meet with you, and share real life time with you. By turning your attention away from them you are inevitably saying "You are not as important." It's really a sickness that we are so addicted to our phones that we ignore the people who are with to hang out with virtual people over Facebook, Twitter, and text messages. Come on guys, it's time to get real.

From my own life, I have realised and understood that the most important aspect of getting yourself away from addiction is just making the decision to change. Sooner or later, most people who have an addiction decide a change needs to happen. Once the decision is made, most people have a specific goal in mind. It might be to quit entirely, to quit some addictive behaviours or substances, but not all, reduce the amount of time or money spent on addictive behaviours, or to reduce the harm of an addictive behaviour. For example, many heavy drinkers have the goal of just one drink a day, or only drinking socially. Getting clear on your goal before putting it into practice is helpful for success in changing an addictive behaviour. Once you are clear on your goal, you may still need to prepare to change. Preparations include removing both addictive substances from your home and triggers in your life that may make you more likely to use those substances again.

Different people have different experience of quitting. Some find the process liberating and empowering, and feel they can achieve anything. Others find it painful, difficult, and frustrating, sometimes needing many failed attempts before achieving their goal. Still others discover new sides to themselves during the quitting process. But if your mind is strong enough you can get rid of your addictions easily and better than anyone else. Even if your goal was to quit completely, you may decide at some point in the future that you want to be able to occasionally indulge without doing so excessively. This is possible, but it is important to be very clear about what it is you want to do. For example, if you want to be able to have an occasional drink with friends, then you need to be able to have one drink and then stop. Many drinkers find it difficult to quit completely and choose to drink occasionally. If you intend to have one drink and end up having several, you should reassess your goals and what is achievable for you at this time of your life. This might be a new experience for you, and it could be liberating. It could also seem boring and difficult.

CHAPTER

Eight

Overthinking and Meditation

All of us have thoughts running in our mind always. While eating, while drinking water, while taking shower, while sleeping also we keep thinking something or the other. The new generation lifestyle has compelled us to keep thinking always. Problem of overthinking has been eating away this generation. I must say that the youth is being ruined by thoughts. During my 15 years of management career, I have come across several people who are always overthinking. Overthinking has become a disease. I was also addicted to this disease until I touched my thirty. My thinking was always about my career, my bank balance, my health and of course the job that I was doing. I never had a peaceful sleep. That gave me few diseases as well. The real hard time came when I was 31 and I had a slip disc. I was playing cricket and I fell down all of a sudden. I was taken to the hospital; the doctor declared that I had a slip disc. Once I was discharged I came home and my wife made me lie down on the floor as sleeping on the bed was really uncomfortable. My son went out for playing. My wife went out for a walk. I was alone lying on the floor looking at the ceiling. Many thoughts came into my mind, I am only 31 and I had a slipped disc. Doctor told me that I can never ever play cricket in my life. He also said that I have to undergo a surgery to cure my back. That surgery costed around rupees 20 Lakhs then in 2012 and I had only 10 lakh money as my savings of 8 years' career. If I am unable to get up and stand my own, who will take care of me. Will my wife be capable enough to earn the money that I was earning? Will she be capable of bringing up our son and offer him all that I could have offered? In the 30 minutes of time when I was alone, I actually saw hell. I thought God has been unfair to me. God punished me for some mistakes.

For almost a week all these thoughts ate my mind day and night. I was on bed to take rest as advised by the doctor. I had taken leave from my job for 15 days. One day, one of my old friend, Rajiv Sinha paid me a visit. He was very fat and was looking very old when I had met him last. But that day when he came home to see me, I found him very lean, very fit and he was looking younger than ever. I was very excited to see him as he was a very good friend. After a while's chit chat, I was curious to know about his transformation. I asked him what medicines he was taking to regain his youth. He then introduced me to the world of yoga. It is not that I didn't know about yoga then. Both my parents had been practicing yoga for a good number of years. Even though they had advised me to practice yoga, I never took it that seriously. I never bothered to learn the benefits of doing yoga. When Rajiv told me that all the transformation he had in him was purely due to yoga, I had realised what I missed. Rajiv told me that my back can be completely fine in 6 months if I practice yoga. I was unsure though, I thought of giving it a try. My concern was how I would learn yoga. Rajiv said he didn't go to any yoga Guru. Whatever he had learnt was from the YouTube and I can also do the same. I had a lot of questions running in my mind. However, since Rajiv was very confident I decided to start learning about Yoga. I googled it, I watched videos on YouTube and after 2 days prepared myself to start practicing. The more and more I learnt about yoga, I understood my problem of overthinking. I also realised that the entire world has this problem like me.

When I searched on YouTube, I also came across Baba Ramdev and his yoga classes on the Aastha channel daily morning. Slowly I started practicing yoga in the morning. Initially it was very difficult. I thought of quitting many times. But I wanted to stand on my feet again; I wanted to do all that I had missed till the age of 30. I wanted to avoid surgery and most importantly I wanted to hold the cricket bat and play again. This was my biggest motivation. Along with yoga, I was introduced to the universal truth of meditation. My God, I can't explain that world. Meditation opened my eyes and explained me that I was sick of this disease called overthinking. I realised how beautiful this world is through the eyes of meditation. I became a completely different man. My anger and frustrations got subsided substantially. I started looking at life more positively The transformation within me gave me the confidence that I can be fit fully by not taking any medicines. I can be back as a healthy person again. I can play cricket. That 15 days' period when I was on leave, I was practicing yoga and meditation. I got an opportunity to do a deep dive into the human in me. I analysed everything from my childhood and the first thing I promised myself was that I would never overthink under whatever circumstances. I would face life as it comes. I agreed that most of the things that I was thinking, I had no control over it. I was purely wasting time and my energy by overthinking. The overthinking disease I had was consuming me. Because of yoga and meditation, I started looking at life more openly and realistically.

So what does meditation involve? Meditation is nothing but sitting in the right and comfortable posture, identify a subject, which you would like to deeply think on. For some it may be some mantras, for some it may be about their God, for some it may be focusing on their breath. Focus on a particular thing, take away your other thoughts. It helps you concentrate on a particular thing. This kind of concentration is extremely important in today's world. In the ancient times, our Saints used to meditate for years. In Hindu mythology, it is believed that, Saints used to worship and meditate to see their God. When you meditate you become selfless. Your negative thoughts are taken away from you. You find purpose of your life. There are different ways of doing meditation. You should choose the one that suits you. The one that is better for you. The one that give you happiness. Through meditation you can conquer your mind, conquer your thoughts and at the end evolve as a good and happy human being. This is the power of meditation. There is no right or wrong way to do a meditation. Till the time you find happiness, you are taken away from your thoughts, it's all good. Like I mentioned I have been practicing meditation for almost 8 years now. It has made me a stronger and better person. I can differentiate it easily with the day when I have not done meditation. It is really a bad feeling and a bad day.

While doing meditation it is important that you will sit in a very relaxed position. If you don't do so your mind will keep getting distracted. One of the things that I do is I chant Mantra "Om". Even though we Hindus consider it as a Mantra there is no religion to "Om". As per the Hindu mythology it is a Universal sound. As per science chanting "Om" create vibrations in your body. I can bet if you chant "Om" for nine times, you will feel the difference in your body. There have been days when I have meditated for an hour. Even though there is no stipulated time for doing meditation, it is advised that on a daily basis you should do it for at least 30 minutes. This will help you eradicate your negative thoughts. I know many people who were under depression and had started meditating; they have found immense results out of this. Whenever, I interact with young students, I advise them to practice meditation. This will not only help them get better in their studies, but also help them to look at life from a different angle. That is the beauty of meditation. I am also aware that many people attacked meditation with spiritual life. While it is good, not necessary you should do it. If you can do meditation regularly, I am of the belief that you can attract positivity from the nature, from the universe. It is better to create this as a habit and improve on a daily basis.

How do I meditate, I will simply put it for you. I sit in a comfortable poster with my spine straight. You may use a chair if you are uncomfortable to sit on the floor. The area where you meditate should be noise-free ideally. This helps you concentrate faster and easier. You should inhale deeply in a way that you sink yourself into the floor. While you inhale you should feel the oxygen getting inside your body. You should be able to concentrate on that movement. You should exhale in a way your shoulders are able to release down the back. You should concentrate and observe how you are releasing the air from your body. Your chin should tilt slightly downward. There are various Mudra. Each Mudra has different purpose. While some Mudra gives you the power to sleep, some can help your digestion faster. You need to identify which Mudra suits you the best. You can also change on a daily basis when you meditate. You should close your eyes while you meditate. Notice as your awareness come gently to the flow of the breath. You can feel the sensation in your body. You can feel the changes that happen in your body. Your body becomes light. You should feel the inhale and exhale process. Allow the breath to flow naturally in a particular rhythm. You should be able to visualize whatever you want to think. It is a very soothing feeling. When I meditate I generally think about my gods that I worship. I feel like they are giving me confidence. I feel like they are blessing me. This boosts my confidence. This gives me strength to fight with the problems of my life. This gives me the confidence that I have a saviour. I feel blessed and happy. As the breath flows in and out, you might sense that the breath is flowing in with particles of very subtle and peaceful light and energy. They flow in with the breath, down into your body, and out with the exhalation. You feel like you are in heaven and all your problems are eradicated. You won't be able to see any problems. You can really fly in the air. Through long meditation sessions, I personally believe that you can touch your soul. You can interact with your soul. You can get the purpose of your life. You don't enjoy the distractions while meditating. Hence it is important that you choose the right place. You must have read about our Saints cursing people to who distract them from meditation. This is the kind of bad feeling that you get when you get distracted. So if you choose the right place, right posture, you will have a good time meditating.

If your body is not relaxed, you can never bring awareness to your breath. You feel relaxed and energetic by exercising. Keep observing your breath during your exercise and do not try to control it. Initially you would have a lot of struggle. So do it very slowly in the beginning. Get the feel of it. Gradually you will learn and improve. Your body will get adapted and accepted. Whenever you want to come out of the meditations state do it very gently. Don't be Harsh with your body. Once you are out of the meditation state, observe the positive energy within you and around you. I can't narrate that feeling. It is an awesome experience.

Let me now explain what can meditation do for stress management. Whenever we experience stress our body automatically reacts in two ways. It either tells us to fight or run away from the situation. When you meditate it affects your body positively and triggers body's relaxation method. It helps your body to become calm. It helps your body to repair itself. It protects your body from further damage. It not only helps your body but it also keeps your mind strong. So, it is a dual benefit when you meditate. Meditation controls your thoughts apart from your body. It brings positive vibes to your body. It gives you energy to fight with any negative circumstance. It strengthens your immune system. With regular practice of meditation, your body and mind both will become stronger. You would be able to fight with any negative circumstances in your life. This is the biggest advantage of meditation. I would advise my readers to practice meditation as a daily habit. It not only keeps you mentally fit but also physically fit.

Let me tell you a real life story of one of my friend. She is older than me by almost 15 years. She was suffering from cancer last stage. She had undergone multiple chemotherapy sessions. She was suffering from severe pain. Doctors tried everything that they could. There was no improvement. Doctors finally advised her family to get her home. Her family started calling all her relatives. Ironically she also wanted to die. She was in tears most of the time. She wanted to quit. This was in 2013. All her relatives started visiting her. One day, one of her visitors advised her to practice meditation. However, my friend was very negative about it. She had practically lost all her hope. She was waiting for the death to embrace her. Through frequent interactions, this visitor convinced her that, she would die smoothly if she practices meditation. He advised her that she can see God before death. This brought a change in your mind. Initially, he advised her to only practice meditation for two hours morning and evening lying on the bed. She found it difficult in the beginning. However, since she had nothing else to do, she decided to pursue it. Initially she wanted to start with 15 minutes. Those 15 minutes in few days became 30 minutes. She kept on increasing.

Slowly her body started getting adapted to it. She could feel the difference both in her body and mind. She decided to do it regularly for 6 hours a day. She started doing it in the morning, afternoon and evening. She found happiness in it. Her pain started reducing. She was feeling better. Her doctor was surprised with the improvements and positive changes in the body. Her family found a ray of hope. Within six months of her practice, she was completely fine. Her pain vanished. This introduced her to the world of Pranayam and Yoga. In a span of another 6 months she was completely fit. She stopped all her medicines fully.

Today she is a yoga teacher and a big inspiration to many. This is what meditation can do to your body. Meditation also strengthens your immunity. It gives your body cells the power to fight against negative circumstances. If you can practice Pranayam and Meditation together, that is the best thing that you can do to your body and yourself.

I am a follower of Baba Ramdev. I consume many off his products. I find them good. I do not want to advertise Baba Ramdev here that's not the objective. He has helped me learn Pranayam and Yoga through the sessions that it takes on TV. I and my wife have learnt through it. I have recommended it to many of my friends. Pranayam has to be a routine affair in one's life, I am of that belief. It increases your oxygen intake and at the same time removes the bad gas from your body. It is really helpful to cope up with many health issues like acidity, breathing issues etc. The best time to do Pranayam is in the morning. Ideally you should do it in empty stomach. Most of your diseases will vanish. You would build a healthy body for yourself. I generally practice Pranayam for 30 to 45 minutes a day. I suggest you should also do it. Meditation is not about becoming a different person or a new person or even a better person, it is.... It is about creating awarness and getting a healthy of perspective. You are not trying to turn off your thoughts or feelings. You are learning to observe them without judgement. When you practice Pranayam you will realise that your journey is more important than your destination. The feeling is that beautiful.

I would urge all my readers start meditating. Start with 5 minutes in a day. Don't stress too much on it. You can do it at your convenience. Either early in the morning or before your bed. If you are not able to concentrate, focus on the God whom you love, think about the God whom you trust, try to see him. The idea is to concentrate. If you don't believe in God, focus on your breath. See how the oxygen is going from your nose to your body. The longer you are able to do it, the better you feel. All your problems like, addiction, overthinking, nervousness, stress and negative thoughts will vanish with the meditation. I have had immense benefit because of meditation. I am sure you too can get it. It will make you a better person, it will make us stronger person and it will make you a beautiful human being. Try it out friends, its worth.

*"Ye Waqt
Gujar Jayega"*